WATER SCIENCE

Active Science with Water

Science Action Labs

Written by Edward Shevick
Illustrated by Marguerite Jones

Teaching & Learning Company
1204 Buchanan St., P.O. Box 10
Carthage, IL 62321-0010

This book belongs to

_____

Cover by Marguerite Jones

Copyright © 1998, Teaching & Learning Company

ISBN No. 1-57310-145-1

Printing No. 987654321

Teaching & Learning Company
1204 Buchanan St., P.O. Box 10
Carthage, IL 62321-0010

Table of Contents
Science Action Labs

Dear Teacher or Parent,

The spirit of Sir Isaac Newton will be with you and your students in this book. Newton loved science, math and experimenting. He explained the laws of gravity. He demonstrated the nature of light. He discovered how planets stay in orbit around our sun.

Water Science can help your students in many ways. Choose some activities to spice up your class demonstrations. Some sections can be converted to hands-on lab activities for the entire class. Some can be developed into student projects or reports. Every class has a few students with a special zest for science. Encourage them to pursue some water science experiments on their own.

Enjoy these science activities as much as Newton would have. They are designed to make your students **think**. Thinking and solving problems are what science is all about. Each section encourages thought. Students are often asked to come up with their best and most reasonable guess as to what will happen. Scientists call this type of guess a **hypothesis**. They are told how to assemble the materials necessary to actually try out each activity. Scientists call this **experimenting**.

Don't expect your experiments to always prove the hypothesis right. These water science activities have been picked to challenge students' thinking ability.

All the activities in **Water Science** are based upon science principles. Many are explained by Newton's laws. That is why Sir Isaac Newton has been used as a guide through the pages of this book. Newton will help your students think about, build and experiment with these activities. Newton will be with them in every activity to advise, encourage and praise their efforts.

The answers you will need are on page 64. You will also find some science facts that will help your students understand what happened.

Here are some suggestions to help you succeed:

1. **Observe carefully.**
2. **Follow directions.**
3. **Measure carefully.**
4. **Hypothesize intelligently.**
5. **Experiment safely.**
6. **Keep experimenting until you succeed.**

Sincerely,

Ed

Ed Shevick

Water Science

Newton Wants You to Know

Water is the main substance in living things. Most living things are at least one-half water. Your own body is two-thirds water.

You couldn't grow and change without water. You couldn't keep your size and shape without water. You couldn't even move without the water in your body.

Water is a **molecule**. It is made of two hydrogen atoms and one oxygen atom. The water molecule is called H_2O.

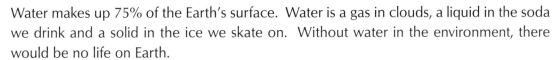

Water makes up 75% of the Earth's surface. Water is a gas in clouds, a liquid in the soda we drink and a solid in the ice we skate on. Without water in the environment, there would be no life on Earth.

1. Place a few drops of water in the palm of your hand.

2. Close your eyes and let your mind dwell on the watery sensation, on your daily need for pure, unpolluted water and on your origin as a minute creature in a warm, drifting sea.

3. Combine your poetic and scientific skills to develop an eight-line poem of great significance.

_____

_____

Water Experiments

Tense Water

The surface of a water drop forms a "skin" that helps the water drop keep its typical shape. Scientists call this **surface tension**. Surface tension explains most of the water drop experiments you are going to do in this lab.

1. Place three different size drops in three different areas of an upside down paper cup. Its waxy surface has very little attraction for water molecules.

Name _____

2. Use a toothpick to roll the drops around. Combine and separate them. Roll them into and away from the cup sides.

3. Describe how your drops react to being pushed around.

_____

_____

Moving Water

Your drops of water appear to be still and motionless. Let's find out if anything is moving inside.

1. Fill the inverted bottom of your cup with water. It doesn't have to bulge upward.

2. Add only one drop of food coloring to one side of the inverted cup.

3. Do not shake the cup in any way. During the next two to five minutes, observe the coloring's movement in the water. What happened to the coloring in the water?

_____

_____

Why did the coloring **diffuse** (spread out) throughout the water?

Newton Hint: What must the individual molecules of water be doing to cause diffusion?

_____

_____

_____

Fun with Water Drops

A drop of water can take many shapes. You are going to observe a few different kinds of drops.

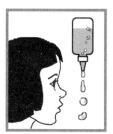

1. Use an eyedropper or dispensing bottle on these experiments.

2. Have a friend form water drops falling by your eyes as shown.

3. Observe the drops carefully both at normal eye level and when they near the ground after a long fall.

6

Name _____

Describe the water shapes you created.

_____

_____

4. Let the drops fall continuously till the individual drops form a stream. Describe what you see.

_____

_____

5. Place your full dropper at eye level. Let some water drops fall from eye level on various surfaces such as wood, glass, metal, tile, etc.

_____

_____

6. Which surfaces gave you the highest water drop bounce?

_____

_____

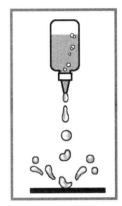

 # Newton Wants You to Measure a Water Drop

Here's one way that Newton knows to measure the volume of a drop of water. It can be done using kitchen materials. This will give you an estimate rather than an exact answer.

1. Hold a teaspoon steady and level on a table.

2. Count the number of drops it takes to completely fill the spoon. Number of water drops to fill a teaspoon. _____

A teaspoon contains 0.17 fluid ounces.

3. Divide 0.17 by the number of drops to find the volume of just one drop.

Example: You counted 30 drops in your teaspoon.

```
        .0056
   30 ) .1700
        150
        200
        180
```

Stop dividing after two numbers beyond the zeros.
One drop = .0056 fluid ounces

3. Follow the example and do the math for your teaspoon experiment.

Your drop = _____ fluid ounces.

Name _____

Water Under Pressure

Newton Wants to Place Both You and Water Under Pressure

Newton loves to solve problems. Here's one of his water pressure favorites.

A milk carton is completely full of water. There are two small holes near the bottom of the carton. Both holes are the **same size** and the **same distance** from the bottom. Water will first be allowed to spurt from only one hole. Then the carton will be refilled, and water will be allowed to spurt from two holes.

What's the Problem?

Will water spurting from one hole travel further than water spurting from two holes? Will they both spurt the same distance? Or will the two holes spurt water further than the one hole?

What Do You Think Will Happen?

Can you give a reasonable explanation for what you predict will happen?

_____

_____

_____

Name _____

How You Can Solve
This Newton Problem

1. Obtain a yardstick (meterstick) and a quart (.95 l) or half-gallon (1.9 l) milk carton.

2. Punch two nail holes about 1" (2.5 cm) from the bottom of the carton. Each hole should be about $^1/_8$" (.3 cm) in diameter. They should be about 1" (2.5 cm) apart.

3. Hold your fingers tightly over both holes, and completely fill the carton with water.

4. Find a convenient place **outdoors**. Place the milk carton on top of an upright yardstick (meterstick). The yardstick (meterstick) is to make sure the milk carton's height above the ground is the same in both experiments.

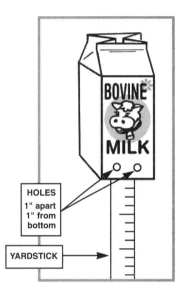

5. Remove **one** finger.

6. Have a friend measure the distance of the one-hole spurt and **quickly** cover the hole with your finger again. _____ inches (cm)

7. Refill the carton so that it is again completely full. This is to make sure the conditions are the same for the two-hole spurt.

8. Place the carton back on the yardstick (meterstick), remove **both** fingers and again measure the spurt distance. _____ inches (cm)

9. It would be a good idea to repeat the entire experiment a few times to be sure of your results.

10. Describe your results.

_____

_____

You will notice that Newton asked you to repeat the waterfall experiment a few times. This is the way all scientists carry on their experiments. Repetition helps avoid errors. It would be a good idea to repeat most of the experiments in this book a few times.

Name _____

Another Newton
Water Pressure Problem

In the previous problem, your milk carton had only two holes at the same height. What would happen if you had three holes, each above the other?

1. Punch nail holes in a line at 1" (2.5 cm), 3" (8 cm) and 5" (13 cm) from the bottom of the carton as shown.

2. Do this experiment **outdoors** or over a sink.

3. Get help to hold fingers tightly over all three holes. Then completely fill the carton with water.

4. Remove all three fingers at the **same** time and observe the results. Repeat the experiment, if needed.

Describe your results.

_____

_____

_____

_____

_____

_____

10

Name _____

Archimedes's Principle—The Buoyant Force of Water

Newton Tries to Explain Archimedes's Principle

Archimedes was an ancient Greek scientist who discovered why corks float and rocks sink in water. Here are the two parts of his famous law.

1. A body **submerged** in water pushes aside its own **volume** of water. **Example:** When you swim underwater, you push aside your body's volume of water.

2. A body **floating** in water pushes aside its own **weight** of water. **Example:** Suppose you weigh 100 pounds (45 kg). If you are floating in water, you are pushing aside 100 pounds (45 kg) of water.

SUBMERGED	FLOATING
PUSHES ASIDE ITS VOLUME OF WATER	PUSHES ASIDE ITS OWN WEIGHT OF WATER

A 100-pound (45 kg) person appears to weigh less than 100 pounds (45 kg) in water. That's because the water that you push aside has an upward **buoyant** force equal to the weight of the water displaced. A 100-pound (45 kg) person appears to weigh only about 80 pounds (36 kg) floating in water.

Eureka, I've lost weight!

Newton Help: Try this the next time you swim. Exhale as much air as possible. Your body **volume** will be **less** and you will sink lower in the water. Take and hold a deep breath. Your body **volume** **expands** and you float higher than usual.

Name _____

Experimenting with Archimedes

The metric system will be used in this activity. In the metric system, the volume and weight of water have a special relationship. One milliliter of water equals one gram of water.

1. Obtain a metric spring scale, a **large**, **heavy** metal bolt and a convenient graduate or measuring cup.

2. Use the spring scale to weigh the bolt suspended in air.

   a. Bolt weight in air _____ grams

3. Use the spring scale to weigh the same bolt while it is submerged **completely** in a graduate. Start with the graduate half filled with water.

   b. Bolt weight submerged _____ grams

   The submerged bolt appears to lose weight due to the buoyant force of the water.

4. Find the weight loss by subtracting answer "b" from answer "a."

   c. "a" minus "b" = _____ grams of weight lost to buoyancy

5. Remove the bolt and adjust the water level in the graduate to somewhere in its middle and record below.

   d. Graduate starting volume = _____ milliliters

6. Lower the bolt again until it is **completely** submerged and record the new volume.

   e. Graduate raised volume = _____ milliliters

7. Find the bolt volume by subtracting answer "d" from "e."

   f. Bolt volume "e" minus "d" = _____ milliliters

Compare your answer in "f" (the bolt's volume) to the answer in "c" (the bolt's loss of weight in water or **buoyancy**). They should be almost the same.

Newton Help: Assume your bolt's volume was 100 milliliters. According to Archimedes's Law, it should be buoyed up (lose weight) equal to the weight of the water displaced or 100. Remember that in the metric system 100 milliliters of water equals 100 grams of water.

Name _____

Archimedes's Puzzler

Floating an Egg

A fresh uncooked egg placed in a glass of water usually falls to the bottom. What can you add to the water to increase its buoyancy and cause the egg to rise?

_____

_____

_____

Floating in Balance

A jar of water and a small block of wood are on the left pan of a balance. The wood block is on the left pan but **not** in the water. Weights are adjusted until the balance is just level as shown at A. Then the block of wood is allowed to float on the water in the jar as shown at B. Will the balance still be level? Explain what you think will happen.

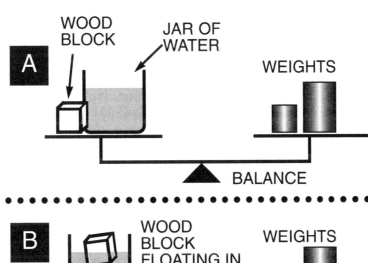

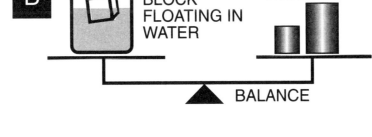

_____

_____

_____

Commanding a Submarine—The S.S. Buoyancy

Newton's Navy Knowledge

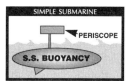

SIMPLE SUBMARINE

PERISCOPE

S.S. BUOYANCY

Did you ever wonder how a submarine moves up and down in the ocean? On the surface, a submarine is like any other boat. It floats because it pushes aside its own weight in water. This gives it buoyancy according to Archimedes's principle.

A submarine allows special internal tanks to flood with seawater when it submerges. The more water in the tanks, the lower the submarine dives. To rise back to the surface, air is pumped into the tanks to remove the water.

Let's build our own demonstration submarine.

Building the S.S. Buoyancy

TRIAL GLASS OF WATER

ADJUST *WEIGHT* OF DIVER SO IT JUST BARELY FLOATS

Making the diver can be done in many ways. You can use a weighted pen top, an eyedropper or a small glass vial.

Now comes the hard part. Use a *full glass of water* to adjust your diver so it **just barely floats**. Adjust the water level in the dropper or glass vial to accomplish this. Use paper clips, modeling clay or wire to help make the weight adjustment. Seal the top of the pen top with clay or tape if it has a hole in it. **Be patient—this part is not easy.**

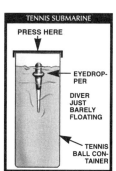

TENNIS SUBMARINE

PRESS HERE

EYEDROPPER

DIVER JUST BARELY FLOATING

TENNIS BALL CONTAINER

1. Fill a plastic tennis ball container with water.
2. Place your barely floating diver *carefully* in the container.
3. Place the container's plastic lid firmly on the top. (You can also use a portion of a balloon secured with rubber bands as a lid.)
4. Press down on the plastic lid to send your diver to the bottom.
5. Stop pressing on the plastic lid and your diver rises.
6. If it doesn't work, your diver is not weighted properly. Try again.

Newton Explanation: When you press on the tennis ball container lid, the air under it presses on the water. This forces water higher up your diver so that it becomes heavier and sinks. When you stop pressing on the lid, the air in the diver expands, pushes out the water, becomes lighter and rises.

14

Weird Water

Newton Wants You to Know

Water is all around and inside us. We take water for granted. Yet water has some weird qualities that make it the world's most interesting matter.

Water Seeks Its Own Level

Observe the drawing to the right. It shows water connected to many different shaped containers.

What is the level of water in all of these containers?

_____

_____

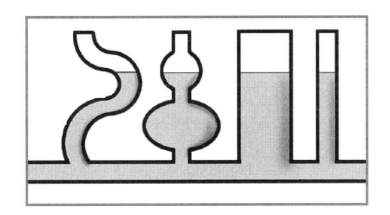

Water Curves

Fill a glass half full of water. Observe the water surface carefully. The water is slightly higher at the edges than in the center. This curve is called a **meniscus**. It forms because water molecules cling to glass molecules better than to each other.

Where Did the Water Go?

Water on a sidewalk after a rain seems to "disappear." Sweat on your body is soon gone. The process by which water returns to the air is called **evaporation**. Evaporation occurs because normal molecules of water are in motion and some fly off into their surroundings.

Name _____

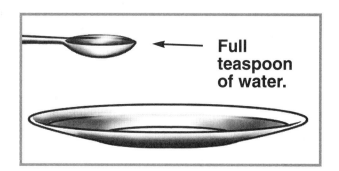

Full teaspoon of water.

Can you speed up the process of evaporation?

Use a full tablespoon of water placed in a small, flat dish as a standard.

List six ways you might be able to speed up evaporation.

1. _____ 2. _____

3. _____ 4. _____

5. _____ 6. _____

Try out your ideas to find the fastest evaporation method. Challenge other students to see who can come up with the best method?

What was the best evaporation method you discovered?

_____

_____

Moving Water

A SIPHON AT WORK

You have probably seen someone empty an aquarium of water using a rubber or plastic tube. This is called a **siphon**. You can demonstrate for yourself how it works.

1. Obtain two large jars and a 3' (.90 m) length of tubing.

2. Fill one jar three-fourths full of water.

3. Place the **empty** jar at least 1' (30 cm) lower than the water jar. See drawing.

4. Place one end of the tubing in the **top** jar.

Name _____

5. Suck on the other end of the tube until it is full of water. You may get some water in your mouth.

6. Pinch the end of the tube with your fingers. Place it into the **lower** jar and release your fingers.

Observe and enjoy your water siphon.

> Siphons can be used to bring drinking water over hills to the cities below. Siphons work because of a combination of gravity pulling on the water flowing downhill in the tubing and air pressure pushing on the water's surface.

Newton Wants You to Have a Paper Towel Race

Besides sticking to other surfaces, water molecules can actually creep through the spaces between many materials. This traveling through materials is called **capillary action**. Capillary action explains how paper towels absorb water and how water moves up through soil to the roots of plants.

Let's observe water's capillary action.

1. Cut a strip of paper towel *roughly* 1" (2.5 cm) wide and 5" (13 cm) long.

2. Fill a glass with water to about 1" (2.5 cm) from the top. Place your paper towel strip so that one end is in the water and the other is bent over the outside.

3. Observe the paper strip for a few minutes.

Describe what you observed in terms of capillary action. Review the top paragraph in this section for help.

_____

_____

Now you are an expert on water's capillary action. Can you use your knowledge to plan an experiment to check the absorption (through capillary action) of different brands of paper towels? The results may surprise you.

A Water Puzzler

Newton's Favorite Water Puzzlers

Your brain is mainly water. Use the water in your brain to solve these water science problems.

Exactly Half Full, Please!

You have a quart (.95 l) jar and all the water you need. You have **no measuring equipment**. All you have are the jar and the water.

How can you fill the jar **exactly** half full of water with no measuring equipment? List your best ideas below.

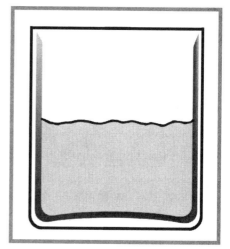

_____

_____

_____

_____

_____

Newton knows one good method for getting the jar exactly half full. He's hoping you'll discover other ways of solving this puzzler. Remember, you have all the water you need but nothing else besides your brain and the jar. When you think you've solved the puzzler, you can use any equipment available to check your results.

Name _____

Empty Me Fast

Newton once worked in a plant that filled small-necked gallon (3.8 l) jars with soda. One day a worker forgot to add the flavoring and 500-gallon (liter) jars of soda were ruined.

Someone had to empty all those gallon (liter) jars into a sink one by one. Naturally, they called on Newton to discover the fastest way to empty the jars. Using Newton's method, they were able to empty each jar in less than 15 seconds.

Can you find a fast method of emptying a jar? Of course, you are not allowed to break the jar. Before actually trying this puzzler, try to think up some speedy ways to empty the jars.

Caution! Be careful doing this experiment so that you don't accidentally drop the jars and hurt yourself. Do the experiment outdoors or over a convenient sink.

There are many ways to approach a science problem. You can use the trial and error method and try various emptying techniques. Or you can start first by thinking and trying to outsmart Newton. Good luck in beating Newton's 15 seconds.

NEWTON'S ACTION LAB
Water Science 7

The Chemistry of Water

Water Is Made of Molecules and Atoms

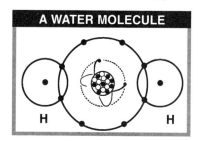

A WATER MOLECULE

H   H

Water is made of tiny particles called **molecules**. A drop of water contains millions of molecules. A tablespoon of water could contain one trillion molecules.

A water molecule, in turn, is made of smaller particles called **atoms**. Water molecules contain two small atoms of **hydrogen** and one larger atom of **oxygen**. The atoms of both hydrogen and oxygen are surrounded by **electrons**. These electrons form the "glue" that holds molecules together.

Some Properties of Water

Water appears on Earth as solid (ice), liquid (water) or gas (steam). The molecules in all forms of water are in constant motion. Slow-moving molecules form ice. Faster molecules break their electron "glue" to form liquid water. Extremely fast molecules escape from liquid water to form steam. Water is the only substance on our Earth that is naturally found as a solid, liquid or gas.

Water in the metric system was selected to have a **density** of one. This means that one cubic centimeter (also one milliliter) of water weighs exactly one gram. Density tells how "heavy" a substance is.

DENSITY TABLE		
(All density numbers compared to water's density of one.)		
SOLIDS	**METALS**	**LIQUIDS**
Bone 2	Aluminum 2.7	Pure Water 1
Brick 1.8	Copper 8.9	Seawater 1.03
Cork 0.2	Gold 19.3	Alcohol 0.8
Ice 0.92	Iron 7.8	Glycerine 1.3
Marble 2.7	Lead 11.3	Milk 1.03
Paraffin 0.9	Silver 10.5	Turpentine 0.9
Rubber 1.2		Mercury 13.6
Bamboo 0.3		
Oak Wood 0.7		
Pine Wood 0.6		

Any substance having a density less than one will float on water. Any substance having a density **greater** than one will sink.

The Chemistry of Water

Name _____

Study the density table.

Name five substances that will float on water.

_____, _____, _____, _____, _____

Name five substances that will sink in water.

_____, _____, _____, _____, _____

What is the least dense substance in the density table?_____

What is the most dense substance in the density table? _____

Water: The Great Dissolver

Sugar **dissolves** when you place it in lemonade. The sugar molecules disappear in the spaces between water molecules. You can taste the sugar but you can't see it.

How Sweet It Is

1. Obtain two glasses and lots of sugar.

2. Fill **both** glasses with the **same** amount of water. One glass will be your experiment control.

3. **Carefully** and **slowly** add up to four level teaspoons of sugar into one glass.

4. Observe the level of water in the sugar water and the control water.

   Are there any differences in the level of the water in each? _____

   Where must the sugar molecules have gone? _____

   _____

   _____

5. Name eight substances that dissolve in water.

   1. _____   2. _____   3. _____

   4. _____   5. _____   6. _____

   7. _____   8. _____

Name _____

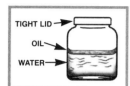

Mixing Oil and Water

1. Obtain a small jar with a **tight lid**, some cooking oil and some dishwashing liquid.

2. Place a small amount of cooking oil into a jar half full of water. What does the oil do?

Newton Hint: Oil is less dense than water. Think of what happens when a tanker spills oil into the ocean.

3. Place the lid firmly on the jar and shake vigorously.

4. Wait a few minutes and observe the liquids. What happened when you stopped shaking the mixture? _____

_____

5. Now add a few drops of dishwashing liquid.

6. Place the lid on **firmly** and again shake vigorously.

7. Wait a few minutes and observe the mixture. Describe what you see. _____

_____

Soap breaks oil into small particles that remain suspended in the water instead of rising. That's one way that soap removes oily substances when you wash your clothes.

Newton Mixes Alcohol and Water

You've heard that drinking alcohol and driving don't mix. Newton wants you to try mixing alcohol and water.

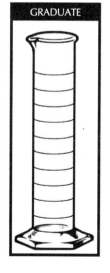

1. Obtain rubbing alcohol, a 50-milliliter graduate and a 100-milliliter graduate.

Caution: Rubbing alcohol is a **poison**. It is not made for drinking.

Hint: If you can't obtain graduates, substitute clear kitchen measuring cups.

2. Measure out **exactly** 50 milliliters of water and place it in the 100-milliliter graduate.

3. Measure out **exactly** 50 milliliters of alcohol and add it to the 100-milliliter graduate.

4. Let it stand without any shaking for three minutes.

5. Measure the combined alcohol and water mixture. _____ milliliters

6. You lost some volume. Where must some of the alcohol or water molecules have gone?

_____

Newton Fact: Alcohol molecules are larger than water molecules. Most scientists think that water molecules find their way into spaces between the alcohol molecules.

Tense Water

Both Newton and Water Have a Skin

Water is made of many molecules that attract each other. The molecules have an especially strong attraction at the surface of water. This attraction is called **surface tension** and acts like a "skin" at the water's surface.

POND SKATER

You have probably seen this "skin" in nature. Insects, such as pond skaters, can actually land and move on top of water without sinking.

Let's observe surface tension directly.

1. Punch four or five holes in a metal or plastic jar lid using a **large** nail.

2. Pour water into the lid until it stops running out the holes.

3. Observe the water skin that forms over the holes.

Describe what you see.

JAR LID WITH
NAIL HOLES

_____

_____

Surface Tension Experiments

Bulging Water

You are going to use water's surface tension to make it bulge out like a fat stomach.

1. Fill the inverted bottom of a paper cup completely with water.

Name _____

2. Use a dropper to keep adding more and more drops until the water surface bulges upward above the top of the cup.

What makes the water bulge upward instead of running over the side of the cup?

_____

_____

Floating Paper Clip

Thanks to surface tension, you can float a metal paper clip on water.

1. Fill a cereal bowl with water to within ¹/₂" (1.25 cm) of the top.

2. Place a small paper clip across the prongs of a fork.

3. Lower the fork and paper clip **slowly** and **carefully** into the water. If done right, the paper clip should float on the water's surface.

Newton Hint: The water, bowl, fork and paper clip should be as clean as possible. The oil from your fingers could disturb the skin at the water's surface.

Breaking Up Surface Tension

Detergents and soap do their cleaning job by breaking up water's surface tension.

Circle of Thread

1. Fill a cereal bowl with **clean** water.

2. Tie a 6" (15 cm) piece of thread or string into a loop.

3. Place the loop in the clean water without touching the water with your fingers.

4. Use a clean toothpick to form it into any **noncircular** shape with an opening in the center.

5. Touch the center of the loop with the end of a toothpick which has been dipped into liquid detergent.

Describe what happened to the thread.

_____

_____

24

Name _____

Surface Tension Boat

You can power a small paper boat using surface tension. Don't try this with a cruise ship.

1. Obtain 1¹/₂" (3.8 cm) square of stiff cardboard. File cards or manila file folders work fine.

2. Cut out the shape of a boat as shown. Be sure to cut a small notch in the rear.

3. Place your boat at the side of a bowl or tray of **clean** water.

4. Touch the water at the notch with the end of a toothpick dipped in detergent.

Describe what happens.

_____

_____

Can you explain the forward motion of the boat in terms of surface tension?

_____

_____

Going Further with Surface Tension

Another Battle of the Bulge

1. Fill two glasses to the **brim** with water.

2. Place both on **dry paper towels**.

Challenge someone to a battle of the bulge. Compete to find who can carefully drop the most pennies or paper clips into the glasses **without** water appearing on the paper towels.

Racing Boats

You have already built the standard cardboard boat in this unit. Challenge someone to a boat race in a long flat pan of **clean** water. Limit your boats to a maximum of 2" (5 cm) long. Use any kind of shape, material or design you wish.

May the best sailor win!

Fill to the brim at the start.

pennies

dry paper towel

More Water Puzzlers

Newton Brags About Himself

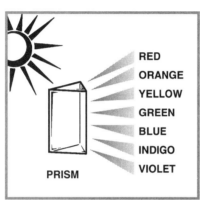

RED
ORANGE
YELLOW
GREEN
BLUE
INDIGO
VIOLET

PRISM

I, Sir Isaac Newton, am one of the world's greatest scientists. I was born in England back in 1642. I received my degree at Cambridge University. In less than 18 months of working at home, I discovered many laws about motion, gravity and light.

My law of light showed that normal light is made of many colors. I used a glass prism to discover this. Oh yes, I invented the prism.

Water particles in the air sometimes act like prisms. That's why you often see a rainbow in the sky after a storm.

Newton Overboard

On Newton's first fishing trip, he fell overboard. Fortunately, Newton was a good swimmer. Saving him became a mathematical problem.

Here's the problem.

1. Newton's arm could only reach 2' (.61 m) above the water's surface.

SS SCIENCE

ROPE IS 4½ FT. ABOVE WATER

NEWTON REACHES UP 2 FEET

Name _____

2. The boat captain threw Newton a rope. Sadly, it was a short rope whose end was $4^1/_2'$ (1.4 m) above the water's surface.

3. The tide was rising 1' (.30 m) every half hour.

4. How long would it be before poor Newton could reach the end of the rope? _____ hours

Water Down the Drain

You have all observed water draining out of a sink or bathtub. You may have observed that the receding water forms a sort of whirlpool.

Some people believe that these whirlpools form counterclockwise in the Northern Hemisphere of the Earth. They also believe whirlpools move clockwise in the Southern Hemisphere. Are you wondering what the poor whirlpools do right at the equator?

Newton challenges you to experiment with your own

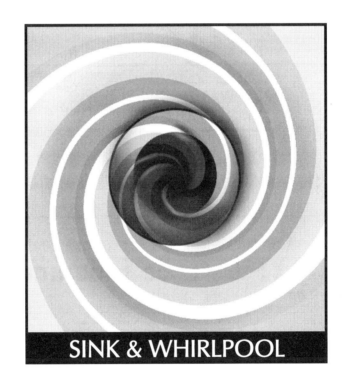

SINK & WHIRLPOOL

sinks and bathtubs. Remember that a good scientist repeats experiments many times before coming to conclusions. Good luck!

What are your conclusions about sink whirlpools?

_____

_____

_____

_____

Name _____

Ice Cube Science

Newton Wants You to Know

WATER MOLECULE

Steam, water and ice contain exactly the same water molecule. The molecule has two atoms of hydrogen and one atom of oxygen. The formula is H_2O.

The real difference between steam, water and ice is molecular motion. Steam molecules move very rapidly, while ice molecules move very slowly. If water at sea level is heated above 212°F (100°C), the molecules move fast enough to boil off as steam. If water molecules are cooled below 32°F (0°C), they form ice.

Ice Cube Experiments

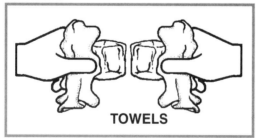

TOWELS

Ice Cube Merger

Combine two ice cubes into one. Use a paper towel to hold two ice cubes firmly together for one minute. The pressure melts the surface which reforms as ice.

Ice Cube Float

Float an ice cube in a **full** glass of water. Part of the ice cube sticks above the glass. Will the glass overflow when the ice cube melts? Wait and see.

Name _____

Observe an Ice Cube in Water

It is like an iceberg floating in the ocean. Most of your ice cube and an iceberg is below the water surface. Can you guess what percentage of your ice cube (or an iceberg) is below the water?

Expanding Ice

Ice expands as it freezes. You can demonstrate this by filling a small milk carton **completely** with water. Place it in the freezer overnight and observe any change.

Newton Fact: Water is strange. As it cools to 39°F (3.9°C), it contracts like any normal substance. As it goes below 39°F (3.9°C), water begins to expand. Water freezes at 32°F (0°C) and continues to expand as its temperature is lowered. The fact that ice floats keeps the ocean bottom from being perpetually frozen.

Newton's Ice Cube Challenge

Newton wants you to build a container that will keep ice cubes from melting as long as possible. Compete with your friends or classmates.

Obtain two regular ice cubes. Pack them with insulating materials in a standard **one-pound** (.45 kg) coffee can. Cover with the plastic lid.

You can use any kind or combination of insulating materials that you wish. Time how long it takes the ice cubes to disappear. The longest lasting ice cube wins.

**COFFEE CAN
1 pound**

The Great Ice Cube Meltdown

Newton's Puzzler Description

Newton once gave a party for 50 youngsters. He wanted to serve iced punch to all his guests. To save time, Newton decided to have the punch glasses poured **before** the party. He worried about the ice melting too soon and the punch becoming too warm. He couldn't decide what to do, so he tried an experiment. He filled one glass with **both** the ice cubes and punch. He filled another glass with **only** ice cubes so he could pour the punch in later.

Which ice cubes do you predict will last longer?

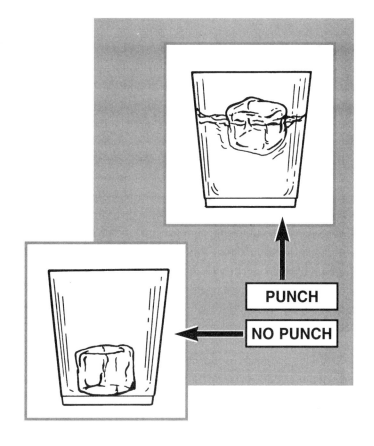

PUNCH

NO PUNCH

Name _____

How to Test Newton's Puzzler

1. Find two glasses that are **exactly** alike.

2. Find two ice cubes that are as alike as possible.

3. Place one ice cube in an empty glass.

4. Place the other ice cube in a glass three-fourths full of water taken directly from the tap.

5. Wait patiently for the ice cube meltdown.

Describe the results.

_____

_____

_____

Newton Wants You to Do More with Ice Cubes

Ice Cube Meltdown Variations

1. Will an ice cube melt faster in oil or water?

2. Will an ice cube melt faster in a full or half full glass of water?

3. Will an ice cube melt faster in front of or away from a fan?

4. Will an ice cube melt faster in plain or salty water?

Think of your own idea.

Will an ice cube _____?

Ice Cube Fun

1. Can you make a multicolored ice cube?

2. Can you make a round ice cube?

3. Can you make an ice cube with a hole through its center?

4. Can you make a miniature igloo of ice cubes?

Name _____

Purifying Polluted Water

How Our Water Gets Polluted

Many kinds of pollution find their way into water supplies. Pollution can be from plants and animals as well as man. Practically every American harbor, river or lake is polluted to some extent.

There would be no problem if the water we used returned unpolluted to the lakes, rivers and oceans. Unfortunately, the water used in our homes ends up as sewage carrying human wastes and soapy chemicals. Used factory and farm water carries with it poisonous chemicals, organic wastes, heat and bacteria. As our population grows, our water pollution problems also grow.

The sentences below refer to key words in our fight against water pollution. Unscramble the bold-faced words.

1. Pollutants that flow out of your home. **wagsee** _____

2. Used to kill bacteria in drinking water. **rolchnie** _____

3. A pollutant spilled from tankers. **loi** _____

4. Rain that falls through polluted air. **daci** _____

5. Found in water that runs off farms and gardens. **sipcideset** _____

6. A form of household soap that can pollute water. **enetgdtre** _____

Name _____

Helping Mother Nature Purify Water

Nature does most of the job of recycling polluted water. Sometimes water is so polluted people must give nature a hand. That's the only way we can obtain a clean, clear, tasty, odorless and germ-free water supply. Let's investigate some of the ways we can help nature recycle water.

One way water can be renewed is by **sedimentation**. *Sedimentation* means letting gravity pull solid wastes down.

1. Obtain a tall sealed jar of muddy water.

2. Shake the covered jar vigorously.

3. Place the jar on a table. Do not touch the jar for five minutes.

Answer these questions after waiting five minutes. Don't throw away the jar of muddy water. You will need it for the activity on page 34.

Which part of the water is clearer?

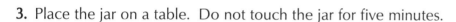

_____

_____

The mud is taking the place of solid water pollutants. What happened to the mud?

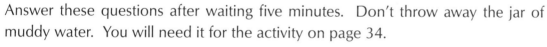

_____

_____

Why wouldn't you drink the relatively clear water at the top of the jar?

_____

_____

Name _____

More Help for Mother Nature

Another way of cleaning water is called **filtration**. *Filtration* means letting water run through something that catches particles. The clear water passes through while the solid pollutants are trapped in the filter.

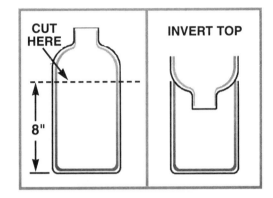

1. Obtain an empty two-liter plastic soda container.

2. Use scissors to cut the top off about 8" (20 cm) from the bottom.

3. Invert the cut-off top and place it in the bottom of the plastic container. It will be your funnel.

4. You are making a polluted water **filter**. Line the funnel with paper towels, tissues, coffee filters, handkerchiefs or "?".

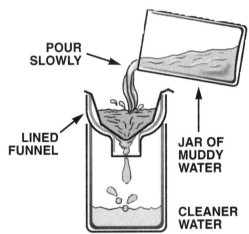

5. Use the same muddy jar you saved from the activity on page 33. Shake it up so that the pollutant (mud) is evenly distributed throughout the water.

6. **Slowly** pour the polluted water through the filter into the plastic bottle. Don't spill muddy water over or around the filter.

Observe the water in the plastic bottle. How does the water compare to the original polluted water?

_____

_____

_____

34

Name _____

Why wouldn't you drink the clear water passing through the filter?

_____

_____

You're right in not wanting to drink the filtered water. Sedimentation and filtration only remove most of the solid pollutants and can leave water with a bad taste and smell. Your filtered water may still contain dissolved chemical poisons or even harmful bacteria.

What doesn't sedimentation and filtration remove from polluted water?

_____

_____

Help Newton–His Pond Is Polluted

Imagine there is a small pond near your home. A tanker truck passing by has an accident. Gallons (liters) of oil spill out and pollute the pond.

How would you go about getting the oil out of the pond? You must hurry or the birds and fish may die. Remember that oil floats on top of water.

List some of the ways you might remove the oil.

_____

_____

_____

If you have the ambition, experiment on a small scale with your ideas. (Pour a little cooking oil into a shallow pan of water.)

THE ALASKAN OIL SPILL

In March 1989, the oil tanker *Exxon Valdez* had an accident. Eleven million gallons crude oil spilled into waters off Alaska. Cleaning up this oil spill took millions of dollars and thousands of man-hours. Many birds, otters, seals, salmon and other creatures were killed.

Name _____

Water Conservation

Newton Loves Percentages

Water is LIFE. Your body is 67% water. A seemingly dry desert plant could be 50% water. Oceans cover 70% of the Earth's surface. Over 97% of all water found on Earth is salty. That leaves less than 3% fresh water available for our use.

About 75% of all fresh water is in the form of ice locked up in ice caps, glaciers and icebergs. Another 20% of fresh water is underground. Only part of this is available through drilling. That leaves only about 5% of the fresh water available in our lakes, rivers and clouds.

Are these percentages giving you the urge to jump into a salty ocean? If so, cure yourself by solving this weird percent problem. Use all percents as "real" numbers and not decimal equivalents.

1. Subtract your body's percent of water from the percent of fresh water locked up as ice.

2. Multiply that answer by the percent of underground fresh water.

3. Divide that answer by the percent of fresh water found in lakes, oceans and clouds.

4. Add the percent of water covering the Earth's surface as ocean.

Your answer is _____.

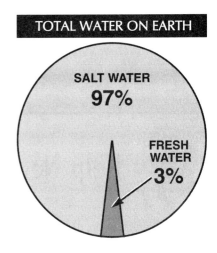

TOTAL WATER ON EARTH

SALT WATER
97%

FRESH
WATER
3%

FRESH WATER ON EARTH

ICE
75%

UNDER-
GROUND
20%

LAKES,
RIVERS and
CLOUDS
5%

Name _____

Where Water Is Used

You consume a lot of water for your personal and home use. You water your lawn and wash your car and dog. You wash your body as well as your clothes and dishes. Here are some facts on how the *average* family uses water.

- **Showers:** about 20 gallons (76 l)
- **Bath:** about 30 gallons (113 l)
- **Flushing a toilet:** about four gallons (15 l)
- **Washing hands or face:** about one gallon (3.8 l)
- **Automatic clothes washer:** about 40 gallons (151 l)
- **Washing dishes for one meal:** about 12 gallons (45 l)
- **Cooking a meal:** about five gallons (19 l)
- **Watering your lawn:** over 120 gallons (454 l)

Our American life-style consumes about 1700 gallons (6426 l) of water per person each day. In some poorer countries, the average person uses only 10 gallons (38 l) per day. You use a lot of water indirectly. Here are some facts that might astound you.

- It takes 150 gallons (567 l) of water to make your Sunday newspaper.
- It takes 200 gallons (756 l) of water to make one automobile tire.
- It takes 300 gallons (1134 l) of water to produce one pound of beef.
- It takes 75 gallons (284 l) of water to grow just one ear of corn.
- It takes 1000 gallons (3780 l) of water to produce one quart (.95 l) of milk.

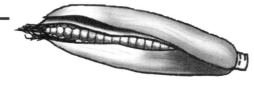

Water Conservation

Name _____

Here are some more water facts. They need your artistic help. Draw objects in the boxes that symbolize a factory, a farm and a home to you.

WATER USE IN THE UNITED STATES

FACTORY USE–50%

FARM USE–40%

HOME USE–10%

Newton Wants You to Save Water

Saving water is important. You can start by saving water right in your own home. Here are a few practical suggestions.

Lawns: Water at night to avoid evaporation.

Washing dishes: Use the dishwasher only when it is full.

Drinking: Keep some water in the refrigerator so you can avoid running the faucet until the water gets cold.

Brushing teeth: Don't let the water run constantly while you are brushing.

Leaks: Check all water appliances for leaks. Even a small leak can run up a water bill.

Driveways: Use a broom instead of a hose to clean the driveway.

All of these are great water-saving ideas. Now it's your turn to develop water-saving ideas. List your four **best** water-saving ideas for the following home areas listed.

Bathroom: _____

_____

_____

_____

38

Name _____

Kitchen: _____

_____

_____

_____

Laundry Room: _____

_____

_____

_____

Garden: _____

_____

_____

_____

Newton's Water Conservation Poster Contest

Let's suppose everyone in the United States used only three gallons (11 l) less water per day. That could save 700 **million** gallons each and every day. You can do your part to save water by entering Newton's poster contest.

1. You can enter three posters.

2. All posters should have a water conservation theme.

3. Emphasis is on saving water at home and school.

4. Each poster should have both a slogan and a drawing.

5. You'll need a clever slogan and a neat poster to win.

6. Find some public place to display your posters.

Name _____

Solving Our Water Problems

Newton's Solutions

Newton wants to remind you that all the water on Earth has probably been around for over four billion years. Nature recycles water over and over again. The same water molecules you drink today may have also been used by ancient Neanderthal people.

You are the solution to water pollution. There is plenty of water in most areas. People have to learn to conserve and not pollute water. We have to find better ways of turning sewer water into reusable **reclaimed** water.

Imagine all the polluted water that flows out of our factories and homes into sewers. In most cities this sewer water is treated by sedimentation, filtration and chemicals to reduce the pollution. Most of the treated sewage water is allowed to recycle back into oceans and lakes.

Reclaimed sewage water is usually unfit to drink. However, this water still can have many valuable uses.

1. Factories use reclaimed water for cooling purposes.

2. Cities use reclaimed water for park and garden watering.

3. High-rise office buildings use reclaimed water to flush toilets.

Put on your thinking cap. Come up with four good ways to use reclaimed water. Remember that it is usually unfit to drink.

_____

_____

_____

_____

40

Name _____

Water, Water, Everywhere and Not a Drop to Drink

About 97% of all the Earth's water is salty. Why not convert the ocean's salty water into pure salt-free water?

Ocean water can and is being desalted. There are many ways to desalt water. However, turning ocean water into fresh water can be expensive. The cost can be up to 10 times more than the cost of normally obtained water.

Purifying Salt Water

Here are some methods used to convert salt water to fresh water.

Distillation

When you boil salt water, the water turns into steam. The salt is left behind. The steam is cooled back into relatively pure water. This system works well but is very expensive.

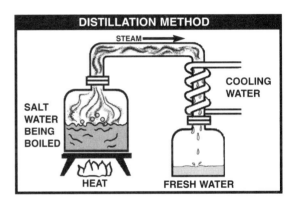

Freezing

Salt water is frozen and then melted. During the process, the salt can be separated from the water.

Electronic

Salt dissolved in water normally breaks into two electronic parts called ions. These salt ions are attracted electrically to special plastic sheets. The salt particles (ions) pass through microscopic holes in the plastic sheets. Water molecules are too big to pass through and stay behind.

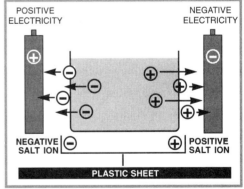

Biological

Some algae (water plant) and some bacteria have the ability to absorb salt. Algae and bacteria can dramatically reduce the amount of salt in seawater.

Name _____

Making Your Own Saltwater Solar Still

1. Obtain a **clean** wide mouth gallon (liter) jar with a lid. You could probably substitute any container with a reasonably large lid.

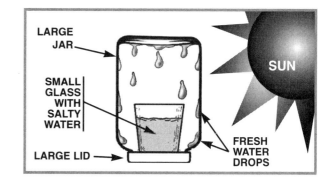

2. Fill a small glass or paper cup with a mixture of salt and water.

3. Place the lid upside down in full sunlight.

4. Place the small glass with salt water in the center of the large lid.

5. Place the jar carefully on the lid as shown. It does not need to be screwed on.

6. Wait at least a half an hour.

Describe what you see forming on the inside surface of the jar.

_____

_____

The sun's heat causes the water, but not the salt, to evaporate. Is the water on the inside surface of the jar fresh or salty?

7. Leave your solar still out a few hours. With a little luck you might end up with a little fresh water in the jar lid. Taste a tiny bit of the lid water. Is it salty?

Newton's Iceburg Solution

Most of the Earth's fresh water is tied up as ice in areas such as Antarctica. Icebergs are considered a water source for the future.

Icebergs range in size from $1/2$ mile (.8 km) to 10 miles (16.1 km) across. A single one-mile (1.61 km) iceberg contains enough fresh water to supply a major city for a month.

Scientists propose towing icebergs to where they are needed. They estimate only $1/10$ would be lost in towing. The icebergs would be stationed near a thirsty city. Parts would be broken off, processed and fed into the city water system.

42

Name _____

Bonus time. The offshore iceberg could also be used as a winter recreation area for skating, sledding and skiing. Can you imagine an iceberg station off Los Angeles, California?

Can you think of any other uses for an offshore iceberg?

_____

_____

Newton's Desert Survival Tip

Plants and animals have learned to adapt to the lack of water in deserts. Gerbils are mouse-sized desert creatures that survive by converting seeds to water. Cactus plants survive by storing water in their stems during the short rainy season.

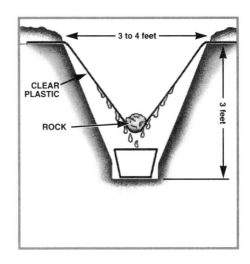

How would you survive in a dry desert? Newton has a clever method of obtaining water. Build his simple solar still. It is based upon the fact that most sand or dirt still has moisture trapped below the surface.

1. Dig a 3' (.9 m) deep circular hole in a convenient dirt area. The diameter should be from 3' to 4' (.9 to 1.2 m) across at the top.

2. Place a collecting container firmly at the bottom.

3. Stretch clear plastic film across the entire hole. Mount the plastic **firmly** by anchoring the plastic edges with dirt or rocks.

4. Place a heavy rock in the center of the plastic. Add additional rocks or weights until the plastic stretches a few inches (centimeters) above the collecting container.

With a lot of sun and a little luck, water drops will form on the plastic and collect in the container.

Caution! Even if your solar still works well, don't drink the water except in an emergency.

Name _____

Water and Weather

Newton Explains the Water Cycle

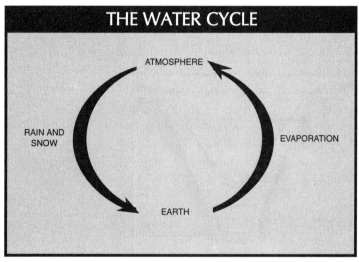

THE WATER CYCLE

The **water cycle** is the movement of water from the Earth to the atmosphere and back again to the Earth.

Water leaves the atmosphere mostly as rain or snow. Water returns to the atmosphere by evaporation. Living things also return water to the atmosphere by perspiration or plant transpiration.

You see this cycle every day. Rain puddles are heated by the sun and evaporate back to the atmosphere. Rain, snow, sleet and hail return water to the Earth.

Here are some amazing water cycle facts.

• Amount of water evaporating from the ocean each year
. . . . .80,000 cu. miles (12,672,000 cu. meters)

• Amount of water evaporating from land each year
. . . . .15,000 cu. miles (2,376,000 cu. meters)

• Amount of water constantly moving between the Earth and the atmosphere
. . . . .95,000 cu. miles (15,048,000 cu. meters)

• Average rainfall on Earth per year . . . . .26" (65 cm)

• Most rainfall per year (in places like rain forests)
. . . . .400" (1000 cm) or 33' (9.9 m)

What is the average rainfall per year where you live? You may have to do some research. _____ average yearly inches (centimeters)

What is the average snowfall per year where you live? _____ average yearly inches (centimeters)

For your information, 10' (25 cm) of snow is considered to be equal to 1" (2.5 cm) of rain.

Name _____

Understanding Clouds

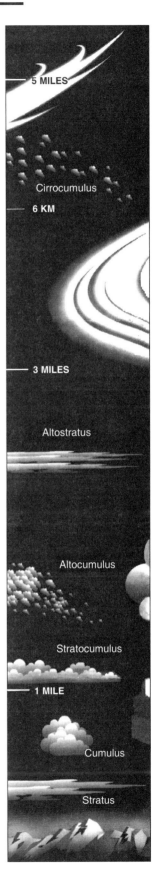

Clouds are often objects of beauty in the sky. Sometimes, as with thunderclouds, they can be threatening objects. Clouds sweep across the sky in a constantly changing pattern and can take an almost infinite variety of shapes. Clouds mirror the present weather and can be used to forecast future weather.

Clouds form when the water vapor in the atmosphere is cooled and condensed into tiny visible droplets of either water, ice or both. Clouds are identified according to their shape, altitude, color and size.

The *simplified* cloud chart on the right will identify the majority of clouds you may view. Notice that it shows high, middle and low clouds. The high clouds often contain the word *cirrus* and are about five miles (8 km) high. The middle clouds often contain the word *alto* and are about three miles (5 km) high. Low clouds often contain the name *stratus* and can range from Earth level (in which case it is called a fog) to one mile (1.61 km) high.

Clouds have three basic forms or shapes. **Cirrus** clouds are high altitude clouds that are made of ice crystals. They have a delicate wispy appearance and bring fair weather. **Cumulus** clouds result from warm, moist air rising and may turn dark and result in rain. The word *cumulus* means "piled up" and many of these clouds have shapes like cotton balls. **Stratus** clouds are the most stable and are usually quite smooth and are often gray in color. They appear as a smooth, *layer-like sheet* across the lower levels of the sky. If the word *nimbus* is combined with a cloud name, it describes a dark cloud that often signals rain.

Moisture falling from clouds is called **precipitation**. Precipitation can be in the form of drizzle, rain, snow, sleet or hail.

Rain: Water droplets over .02" (.08 cm) in size. Each particle of rain, as well as snow, sleet or hail forms around some type of microscopic dust in the atmosphere.

Snow: Clear or cloudy ice particles form into crystals. Snowflakes form directly from water vapor into ice without becoming liquid first.

Hail: A lump of round or irregular ice that can range from .04" to 4" (.15 to 10 cm) in diameter. Hailstones are made of layers due to their being blown up and down numerous times during a thunderstorm.

Sleet: Ice pellets that form when raindrops fall through a layer of air that is below freezing (32°F [0°C]).

Name _____

Go outside and, hopefully, view some beautiful clouds. Describe the kind of clouds

you see. _____

_____

Poetry time. The moving clouds above should give you an urge to create an eight-

line poem. _____

_____

_____

_____

_____

Newton's Homemade Cloud

Here's how to build Newton's cloud maker.

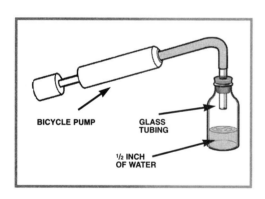

BICYCLE PUMP   **GLASS TUBING**   **½ INCH OF WATER**

1. Obtain a **strong** quart (.95 l) bottle, a one-hole stopper that just fits the bottle, glass and rubber tubing and a bicycle tire air pump.

> **Caution!** Obtain adult help in constructing and operating Newton's cloud maker. Newton's teacher helped him.

2. Construct the device shown. Use water or liquid soap to place the glass tubing in the stopper. **Do not force it in.**

3. Add ¹/₂" (1.25 cm) of water to the bottle. Rubbing alcohol works even better.

4. Press the stopper in the bottle and use your hand to hold it in.

5. Have a helper pump air into the bottle three or more times.

6. Pull the stopper quickly out of the bottle on the last pump. You may not succeed the first time. Be patient and try different methods.

> When you release the air pressure on the water in the bottle, it evaporates quickly. In the real world of the air above you, low pressure is more likely to result in rain.

Name _____

More Water and Weather

Newton on Humidity

Humidity is the term used to describe the amount of water vapor in the air. Humidity determines, to a large extent, how comfortable we are. High humidity keeps our perspiration from evaporating, and we feel "sticky." Too little humidity can be unhealthy.

High humidity can affect your moods. Children have more discipline problems. Many people feel gloomy, sullen and even pessimistic when the air is very moist.

Describe how you feel during very humid days. _____

_____

_____

Measuring Humidity

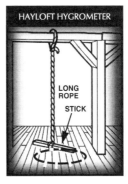

HAYLOFT HYGROMETER

LONG ROPE

STICK

Robert Hooke measured humidity way back in the 17th century using wild oats. He knew that wild oats absorbed and held moisture from the air.

Farmers used to use the hayloft hygrometer shown to the right. A stick is hung from a long rope. When the rope gets moist from humid air, it stretches and twists.

A modern hygrometer uses two thermometers to measure humidity. One of the thermometers is kept dry. The other is kept moist by a wick dipped in water. Readings are taken with both the dry and wet thermometers. The two readings are compared on a standard chart (page 48) which gives the percent relative humidity.

Example: A dry bulb thermometer reads 68°F (20°C). A fanned, wet bulb thermometer reads 60°F (16°C).

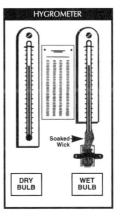

HYGROMETER

Soaked Wick

DRY BULB

WET BULB

Name _____

Treat the humidity data like a multiplication table. Find where the 68 and 60 **intersect**. Your example's relative humidity is 62%.

1. Obtain two thermometers.

2. Wrap a wet tissue around a bulb of one of them.

3. Go outside in a sunny area and take both dry and wet temperatures. Remember to *fan* the wet bulb.

Dry bulb temperature _____°F (°C)

Wet bulb temperature _____°F (°C)

Relative humidity (from chart) _____°F (°C)

4. Repeat your readings in various outdoor and indoor locations.

Location 1 _____ Dry_____ Wet _____ % Humidity_____

Location 2 _____ Dry_____ Wet _____ % Humidity_____

Location 3 _____ Dry_____ Wet _____ % Humidity_____

RELATIVE HUMIDITY CHART

DRY BULB TEMPERATURE

WET BULB TEMP	61	62	63	64	65	66	67	68	69	70	71	72	73	74	75	76	77	78	79	80
41	6	4	2																	
42	10	8	6	4	2															
43	14	12	10	7	5	3	2													
44	18	16	13	11	9	7	5	3	1											
45	22	20	17	15	12	10	8	6	5	3	1									
46	27	24	21	18	16	14	12	10	8	6	4	3	1							
47	31	28	25	22	20	17	15	13	11	9	7	6	4	3	1					
48	35	32	29	26	24	21	19	16	14	12	10	9	7	5	4	3	1			
49	40	36	33	30	27	25	22	20	18	15	13	12	10	8	7	5	4	3	1	
50	44	41	37	34	31	29	26	23	21	19	17	15	13	11	9	8	6	5	4	3
51	49	45	42	38	35	32	30	25	24	22	20	18	16	14	12	11	9	8	6	5
52	54	50	46	43	39	36	33	31	28	25	23	21	19	17	15	13	12	10	9	7
53	58	54	50	47	44	40	37	34	32	29	27	24	22	20	18	16	14	13	11	10
54	63	59	55	51	48	44	41	38	35	33	30	28	25	23	21	19	17	16	14	12
55	68	64	60	56	52	48	45	42	39	36	33	31	29	26	24	22	20	18	17	15
56	74	69	64	60	56	53	49	46	43	40	37	34	32	29	27	25	23	21	19	18
57	78	74	69	65	61	57	53	50	47	44	41	38	35	33	30	28	26	24	22	20
58	85	79	74	70	66	61	58	54	51	48	45	42	39	36	34	31	29	27	25	23
59	89	84	79	74	70	66	62	58	55	51	48	45	42	39	37	34	32	30	28	26
60	94	89	84	79	75	71	66	62	59	55	52	49	46	43	40	38	35	33	31	29
61	100	94	89	84	80	75	71	67	63	59	56	53	50	47	44	41	39	36	34	32
62		100	95	90	85	80	75	71	67	64	60	57	53	50	47	44	42	39	37	35
63			100	95	90	85	80	76	72	68	64	61	57	54	51	48	45	43	40	38
64				100	95	90	85	80	76	72	68	65	61	58	54	51	48	46	43	41
65					100	95	90	85	81	77	72	69	65	61	58	55	52	49	46	44
66						100	95	90	85	81	77	73	69	65	62	59	56	53	50	47
67							100	95	90	86	81	77	73	69	66	62	59	56	53	50
68								100	95	90	86	82	78	74	70	66	63	60	57	54
69									100	95	90	86	82	78	74	70	67	63	60	57
70										100	95	91	86	82	78	74	71	67	64	61
71											100	95	91	86	82	78	74	71	68	64
72												100	95	91	86	82	79	75	71	68
73													100	95	91	87	83	79	75	72
74														100	96	91	87	83	79	75
75															100	96	91	87	83	79
76																100	96	91	87	83
77																	100	96	91	87
78																		100	96	91
79																			100	96
80																				100

48

Name _____

Newton's Simple Rain Measuring Device

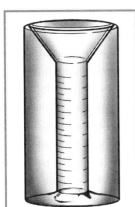

Measuring Rainfall

Shown to the left is a professional **rain gauge**. It is used to measure rain water or melted snow.

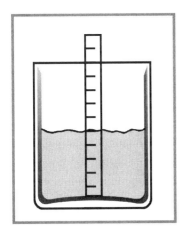

You can easily make Newton's simple rain gauge shown at the left. Set it up in an open space so nothing but sky is above it. Mount it firmly in 1" (2.5 cm) of ground so that it doesn't blow over. Check and record the rainfall each day. Empty each day.

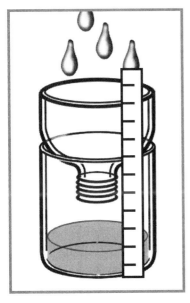

A better rain gauge can be made from a clear plastic $1/2$ gallon (1.9 l) soda bottle. Simply cut off the top and invert it to use as a funnel to trap rainfall.

Snowflakes: Frozen Water

Newton Loves Snow

You have learned that water is part of a cycle. Water on Earth evaporates and rises into the atmosphere. Water from the atmosphere falls as **precipitation**. Precipitation can be in the form of rain, snow, sleet or hail.

Newton wants you to concentrate on snow precipitation in this activity. Here are some facts about snow and snowflakes.

1. Snowflakes always appear as six-sided crystals.

2. No two snow crystals are exactly alike.

3. Some crystals are flat and some form long needles.

4. Snowflakes are really transparent. They appear white because the crystal surfaces reflect light.

5. Snowflakes form in clouds when the temperature is below freezing or 32°F (0°C).

6. Ten inches (25 cm) of snow is considered equal to 1" (2.5 cm) of rain.

7. There have been records of over 1000" (2540 cm) of snow falling in one year.

Making Your Own Snowflakes

Here is a simple way to make your own giant snowflake. As with real snowflakes, no two you make will be exactly alike.

Follow directions **carefully** or your paper snowflake will be a snowflop.

TLC10145 Copyright © Teaching & Learning Company, Carthage, IL 62321-0010

Name _____

1

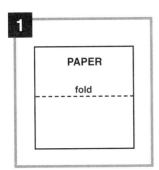

Fold the square exactly in half and crease the middle tightly.

2

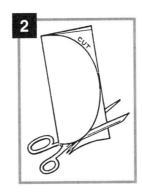

Cut off the corners to obtain a rounded half circle.

3

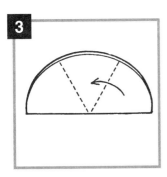

Fold the half circle in **thirds**. This is important. It might help to draw light pencil lines marking the paper into 60° sections before folding.

4

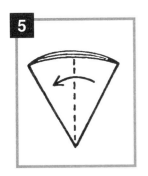

Crease the thirds so that your paper almost looks like a triangle.

5

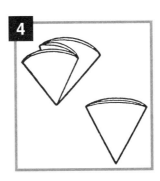

Fold your "triangle" in half.

6

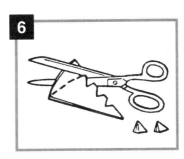

- Cut three notches off the ends as shown.
- Cut the top so that it is circular as shown.

7

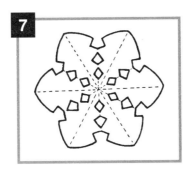

Unfold and enjoy your artistic six-sided snowflake.

Try to devise a better paper snowflake. Change the folds, notches. Good luck!
Remember that real snowflakes are six sided.

Save My Heat

Newton Heat Lecture

Scientists define heat in terms of molecular motion. Hot substances have rapid molecular motion. Cold substances have slower molecular motion. When something "feels" hot, it is because its molecules are doing a rapid dance.

Water is a very unusual substance. You can add more heat to water than to practically any known substance. Consider water a remarkable molecular bank than can take in and store great amounts of heat.

In this activity, you are to compete against your friends and classmates to save the "heat bank" from losses.

Heat Conservation Contest

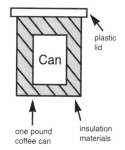

plastic
lid

Can

one pound
coffee can

insulation
materials

Your challenge is to surround a soda can of hot water with materials that will conserve heat. Materials that conserve heat are called **insulators**. You are free to pick and choose any kind or kinds of insulating materials you wish.

1. Obtain an empty soda can and a one-pound (.45 kg) coffee can with a plastic lid.

2. Collect small amounts of insulators of your choice. You will only need enough to fill the small space between your soda and coffee cans.

3. Your teacher or an **adult** will provide you with 200 milliliters or six fluid ounces (177 ml) of very hot (**but not boiling**) water.

4. Every competing student or team will get **exactly** the same amount and temperature of hot water.

5. Use a thermometer to take and record your water temperature. _____ degrees

6. **Carefully** place the soda can in the coffee can. Pack in as much insulating materials as you can. Yes, you can pack insulators on the top and bottom of your soda can.

7. Place your plastic lid on your coffee can.

8. Place all competing cans in the same spot and wait 10 minutes.

9. Open your coffee can and record the water temperature again. _____ degrees

(Do all cans as quickly as you can.)

How many degrees did the water temperature drop in the 10 minutes? _____degrees

Check with your competing teams. Which team had the best insulator and the least heat loss?

Best insulator(s) _____   Degrees lost _____

Congratulations! You have learned how to conserve heat by insulators. Could you plan a competition around how best to keep ice cubes from melting?

Still Another Water Puzzler

Which Way Will It Move?

A cork is floating in a large jar of water. It is kept in the center of the jar of water by a string tied to it and attached to the lid. The entire jar is given a **quick**, **sharp shove** along a tabletop.

What's the Problem?

What will be the **first** motion of the cork when the jar is given the quick, sharp shove? Will the cork remain centered in the jar? Will the cork move forward in the same direction as the shove? Or will the cork move backward in the jar in a direction opposite of the shove?

> Newton fools most people with this puzzler. Before you read the answer key, think of what happens when you are in a car that suddenly moves forward. How is the cork in the jar of water different than you in a car?

What Do You Think Will Happen?

What is your prediction? _____

_____

Can you give a reasonable explanation for your prediction? _____

_____

_____

Name _____

How to Build Newton's Puzzler

Obtain a cork, string, thumb-tack and a large jar with a tight lid.

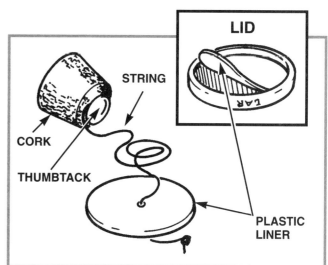

1. Cut a piece of string that is about the length of the jar.

2. Attach one end of the string to the small end of the cork with the thumb-tack.

3. Remove the plastic liner from the inside of the jar lid.

4. Poke a small hole in the center of the liner. **Note:** The hole is not in the lid of the jar.

5. Push the other end of your string through the hole. Tie a bulky knot in the string so that it can't pass back through the liner.

6. Reinsert the liner tightly in the lid.

7. Fill the jar almost full of water and screw the lid on **as tight as possible**.

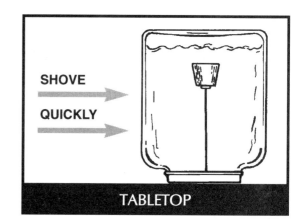

8. Invert the jar on a sink and check for leaks. The top of the cork should be floating at least 1/2" (1.25 cm) below the surface of the water. If it isn't, adjust the length of the string at the cork or add more water.

9. Give the jar a quick, sharp shove along a table. Observe the **first** motion of the cork when shoved.

10. **Caution!** Take care not to push the jar off the table.

Chromatography: Art with Moving Water

Newton Explains Chromatography

Chromatography means "to write with color." Scientists use chromatography to separate mixed-up molecules. The process uses water passing through absorbent paper to separate the molecules by weight. The lightest molecules move the most. The heaviest molecules move the least.

Experimenting with Chromatography

1. Obtain a few small glasses or paper cups.

2. Fill them three-fourths full with water.

3. Obtain some high-quality **white** paper towels.

4. Cut rough circles out of them. The circles should stick out nearly 1" (2.5 cm) on all sides of the paper cups or glasses used.

5. Cut a 3/4" (1.9 cm) strip to the **center** of the circles as shown. *Do not cut* the strip at the center. Bend the strip so it hangs down.

6. Obtain various colors of felt pens or food coloring.

7. Place a generous dot of color on one paper circle right above the bent strip at the point shown.

8. Try combining pen or food coloring on some of the other paper strips.

9. Place the paper circles over the glasses with the bent strips extending into the water.

10. Wait five to 10 minutes and observe your results.

Describe what the moving water did to the color pigments (molecules)

_____

_____

Would the colors at the circle's edges have the heavier or lighter pigments?

_____

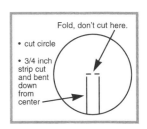

Name _____

Water and Life

Newton Wants You to Know

Human beings could not exist without water. Animals cannot live without water. Without water, there would be no plants. Water is basic to all life on Earth.

In a world without water there would be no clouds, rain or snow. Can you imagine a beach without water or surfers?

List five things you would miss the most in a world without water.

1. _____

2. _____

3. _____

4. _____

5. _____

Water for Your Body

Your body weight is about two-thirds water. You can live longer without food than you can without water. Losing 10% of body water can often be fatal.

Normally you need about 1¹/₂ quarts (1.4 l) of liquid each day. You may not have to drink 1¹/₂ quarts (1.4 l), for many solid foods contain the water you need.

Let's try to roughly estimate your liquid intake for one full day. You can measure either in liquid ounces **or** metric milliliters. Here are some liquid conversions you may need. They are **rounded off** for convenience.

A standard kitchen paper cup = ¹/₃ pint = 5 ounces = 150 milliliters

A pint = 16 ounces or 475 milliliters

A quart = 32 ounces or 950 milliliters

56

Name _____

Most products tell you the volume on the label. When needed, use a basic five ounce (148 ml) paper cup to measure your intake. You will find the One Day Water Intake Chart below.

Type of Liquid	Volume of Liquid	
	Ounces	Milliliters

Newton Wants to Stretch Your Mind

Charge Your Imagination

There may be a serious water shortage some time in the future. What could be done to cut down on the use of water?

GERBILS SURVIVE IN DESERTS

_____

_____

_____

_____

_____

Living Without Much Water

Some plants and animals survive desert life with a minimum of water. Research how cactus, desert plants, gerbils and snakes survive in deserts.

Name _____

Water and Your Body

Newton Loves Water

Water Guessing Game

Newton wants to impress upon you how vital water is to your good health. Use the words in the box to complete the health sentences below.

tears	bones	muscles	cells	nose and mouth
kidneys	brain	eyes	skin	stomach and intestines

1. Water makes up four-fifths of the _____ that help you move.

2. Water makes up one-fourth of the_____ that hold you upright.

3. The body signals the _____ that you are thirsty.

4. Water sweats out of the pores of your _____.

5. Your eyes produce watery _____ when they are irritated.

6. You see by means of two water-filled bags called_____.

7. About one-third of the water in your body is inside your billions of _____.

8. Water is needed by your _____ to form urine and remove wastes from your body.

9. The inside of your _____ moistens the air you breathe.

10. Water helps dissolve food in your _____.

Name _____

Dry Mouth Time

Obtain two crackers. Chew them slowly using as little of your saliva as possible.
No water allowed!

Describe how your mouth feels.

_____

_____

> Saliva, of course, is mostly water. Saliva also begins the process of digestion by changing starch into sugar.

How Water Leaves Your Body

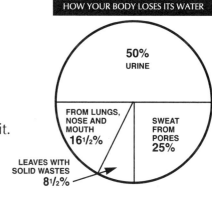

HOW YOUR BODY LOSES ITS WATER

50%
URINE

FROM LUNGS, NOSE AND MOUTH
16½%

SWEAT FROM PORES
25%

LEAVES WITH SOLID WASTES
8½%

Study the chart on the right. It shows how water leaves your body.

Breath Water

1. Place a dish in the refrigerator for 10 minutes.

2. After 10 minutes, hold the dish near your mouth and breathe on it. What do you see forming on the cold dish?

Where must this moisture have come from?

_____

_____

How Water Leaves Your Pores

1. Obtain a clear plastic bag and some tape.

2. Place the bag over your hand and tape it, but not too tightly, as shown.

3. Wait 10 minutes. What do you see forming inside the plastic bag?

How did this water leave your body?

> Losing water through your skin serves two purposes. It eliminates wastes and cools your body to help maintain your normal 98.6°F (37°C) temperature.

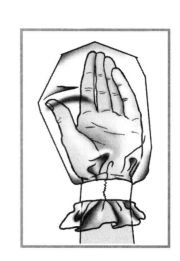

Name _____

How Water Enters Your Body

Study the graph on the right. It shows how water enters your body. Over 62% of your water needs are met by drinking fluids. Around 25% comes from the water found in solid foods. You may be surprised to learn that the cells of your body manufacture over $12\frac{1}{2}$% of your body water needs.

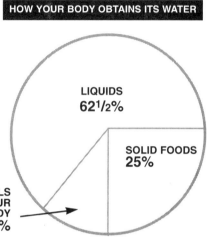

HOW YOUR BODY OBTAINS ITS WATER

LIQUIDS
$62\frac{1}{2}$%

SOLID FOODS
25%

MADE BY CELLS
INSIDE YOUR
BODY
$12\frac{1}{2}$%

1. Obtain some dried beans or peas.

2. With the help of an **adult**, heat them in a pan.

Describe what you see coming off the beans. ____

_____

What does this experiment prove is contained in dry beans?

_____

_____

_____

WATER IN SOLID FOODS

Here is a list of five different solid foods. Can you place them in order of their percent of water?

apple   lettuce   hot dog   bread   egg

Most Water ◄- -► Least Water

1. _____

2. _____

3. _____

4. _____

5. _____

60

Plants Need Water

Newton Wants You to Know

Your blood circulates within you. That means that blood makes a continuous trip from your heart to all parts of your body and back again. Blood, of course, is mostly water.

Plants also use water. The method by which water moves in a plant is called **transpiration**. Transpiration is a **one-way** trip from the roots, up the plant and out through holes in the leaves.

Transpiration keeps plants cool and moves materials absorbed by the roots up through the plant. The leaves of a plant let most of the water evaporate into the air. Leaves have **stomates** (a Greek word for "little mouth") that open or close as transpiration is needed. The drawing to the right shows leaf stomates.

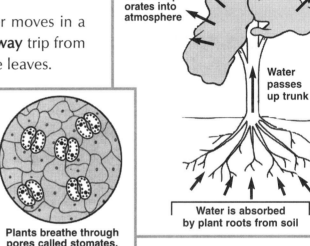

PLANT TRANSPIRATION

Water evaporates into atmosphere

Water passes up trunk

Water is absorbed by plant roots from soil

Plants breathe through pores called stomates.

Plants Take in Water

Most animals use a heart to pump blood. Plants move water up without a pump. Newton wants to demonstrate this water elevator using celery.

1. Obtain a tall glass, a fresh stalk of celery and food coloring.

2. Cut across the celery stalk near the bottom.

3. Fill the glass half full of water and add **lots** of food coloring.

4. Place the glass in a warm area overnight.

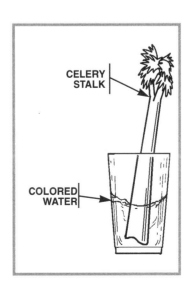

CELERY STALK

COLORED WATER

Name _____

Describe how your soaked celery looked.

_____

_____

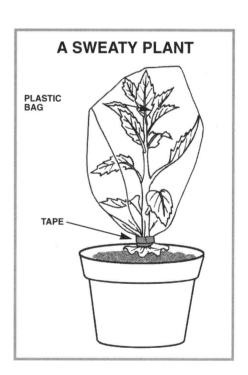

5. Cut the celery stalk near the bottom again. Observe the celery cross section and describe what you see.

The colored dots in the stalk show that only the pipe-like structures are moving water upward.

Newton's Challenge: Obtain a white flower such as a carnation. Can you use what you've learned to change its color? Could you make it multicolored?

Plants Give Off Water

Animals perspire to keep cool. So do plants. Here's how you can "see" plants sweating.

1. Obtain a small, leafy potted plant.

2. Place a clear plastic bag over the plant as shown. The plastic bag **should not** cover the dirt. Seal the bag with tape as shown.

3. Place the plant where there is plenty of **light** and wait for at least an hour.

What do you see inside the plastic bag that wasn't there before?

_____

What *part* of the plant must have given off the water?

_____

A SWEATY PLANT

PLASTIC BAG

TAPE

Newton's Special: Try this experiment to be sure the water came from the leaves and not the stem. Strip your plant of **all** of its leaves and repeat the experiment with a **dry** plastic bag.

Name _____

Newton Tells You More About Plants

Plants use water in many ways. Water cools plants and moves minerals and food up and down. Plants also use water for a process called **photosynthesis**.

Photosynthesis turns plants into food factories. Plants use water and carbon dioxide as raw materials. They use sunlight as an energy source. The plant factory manufactures sugar and oxygen.

Leaves could not act as sugar factories if they did not contain a green pigment called **chlorophyll**. It is the chlorophyll that converts water and carbon dioxide to sugar and oxygen.

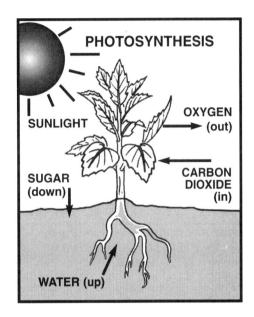

PHOTOSYNTHESIS

SUNLIGHT

OXYGEN (out)

SUGAR (down)

CARBON DIOXIDE (in)

WATER (up)

Newton wants you to extract chlorophyll from leaves.

1. Obtain some rubbing alcohol, fresh green leaves and a small jar.

2. Tear the leaves into small sections and place in a jar one-fourth filled with alcohol.

3. Check the alcohol color after an hour of soaking.

RUBBING ALCOHOL

TORN LEAVES

What pigment did alcohol remove from the leaves? _____

What do you think would happen if you repeated this experiment with water

instead of alcohol? _____

WATER FACTS

Transpiration can move water to the top of a 300' (90 m) redwood tree. A single corn plant can sweat two quarts (1.9 l) of water every day. Hydroponics is a method of growing plants without soil. Hydroponics soaks plant roots with enriched water.

Answer Key

Another Newton Water Pressure Problem, page 10

The water from either one or two holes in the first experiment will spurt out the same distance. How far the water spurts depends only on the height of the water in the milk carton. The water's height determines the pressure on the water forced out. Remember how your eardrums feel the deeper you dive in a swimming pool.

Archimedes's Puzzler, page 13

1. Add salt to the water to make it denser. Salt water is more buoyant. You discover this when you swim in the salty ocean.

2. The balance will stay level. Wood, in or out of water, still has the same mass or amount of material.

Exactly Half Full, Please! page 18

Add water to the jar so that it is obviously over half full. Place the jar over a sink. Tilt the jar to slowly pour out the water. Stop pouring when the water surface touches both the top of the jar and the point where the side and bottom join. See the diagram. At this point your jar is exactly half full.

Empty Me Fast, page 19

Air pressure is working against you in this puzzler. It tends to keep the soda in the jar. You must get air inside the jar to help you force the soda out.

Hold the gallon (liter) jug **firmly** with two hands over the sink. Rotate the jar rapidly to form a tornado-like air funnel in the jar. Stop rotating to let the air come in and push the water out.

Newton Overboard, page 27

Newton will never reach the rope. As the tide rises, so does the boat.

Water Down the Drain, page 27

Your whirlpool experiments should show no definite clockwise or counterclockwise spinning. There is just too little water in your sinks and tubs to be affected by the Earth's natural spinning. Most home whirlpools are affected by the shape of the bowl and the motion of the water before the drain is opened.

Large cyclone weather patterns that form over the Earth do form whirls. These cyclones curve to the right in the Northern Hemisphere and to the left below the equator.

How to Test Newton's Puzzler, page 31

The ice cube in water melts much faster. You need some background on heat. Heat is actually a measure of matter's molecular motion. In ice, molecules move slowly. In water, molecules move faster. In steam, the molecules are moving so fast that they can escape into the air.

Heat can move around by radiation, conduction and convection. In our ice cube experiment, the heat moved very slowly from the air into the ice cube. The ice cube in water melted faster because heat moved more rapidly from the water by both convection and conduction.

How Our Water Gets Polluted, page 32

1. sewage, 2. chlorine, 3. oil, 4. acid, 5. pesticides, 6. detergent

Newton Loves Percentages, page 36

102

Still Another Water Puzzler, page 36

The cork will first move forward in the direction of the shove. This may seem contrary to what you experience when a car suddenly moves forward. The law involved here is Newton's Law of Action and Reaction. The law states that for every action, there is an equal and opposite reaction. As you push the jar forward, the water obeys Newton's law and moves backward. The floating cork is acted upon by the water moving backward. The cork also obeys Newton's law by moving in the opposite direction to the moving water. Therefore, it initially moves forward.

Newton Loves Water, page 58

1. muscles, 2. bones, 3. brain, 4. skin, 5. tears, 6. eyes, 7. cells, 8. kidneys, 9. nose and mouth, 10. stomach and intestines

How Water Enters Your Body, page 60

Percent of water: 1. lettuce (96%), 2. apple (85%)

3. egg (74%), 4. hot dog (57%), 5. bread (36%)

TLC10145 Copyright © Teaching & Learning Company, Carthage, IL 62321-0010